Dairy Free]
Cookbook

Easy And Delicious Dairy Free Baking And Dessert Recipes

Table of Contents

Honey Cake

Pumpkin Cake

Peanut Butter Brownies

Molasses Cinnamon Cake

Pear Cake

Citrus Cake

Almond Cake

Zucchini Brownies

Chocolate Cake

Hazelnut Chocolate Cake

Introduction

Lactose intolerance is a very common condition that causes digestive issues for many people. The symptoms of lactose intolerance vary greatly, some people only experience gas and minor abdominal discomfort, but others can experience more severe symptoms like diarrhea and vomiting. If you have lactose intolerance probably know that it can be very difficult finding baked foods that do not have dairy. The good news is that there are plenty of great alternatives to dairy for using in baking.

With these dairy free baking recipes, it is impossible to tell that they do not contain milk or dairy. I have included a wide variety of my favorite dairy free cookie, cake and dessert recipes that anyone can enjoy. Good luck!

Chapter 1: Dairy Free Cookie Recipes

Dairy Free Gingersnap Cookies

Ingredients

2 1/4 cups all-purpose flour

2 teaspoons ground ginger

1 teaspoon baking soda

3/4 teaspoon ground cinnamon

1/2 teaspoon ground cloves

1/4 teaspoon salt

3/4 cup margarine, softened

1 cup white sugar

1 egg

1 tablespoon water

1/4 cup molasses

2 tablespoons white sugar

Directions

Preheat oven to 350 degrees F (175 degrees C). Sift together the flour, ginger, baking soda, cinnamon, cloves, and salt. Set aside.

In a large bowl, cream together the margarine and 1 cup sugar until light and fluffy. Beat in the egg, then stir in the water and molasses. Gradually stir the sifted ingredients into the molasses mixture. Shape dough into walnut sized balls, and roll them in the remaining 2 tablespoons of sugar.

Place the cookies 2 inches apart onto an ungreased cookie sheet, and flatten slightly.

Bake for 8 to 10 minutes in the preheated oven. Allow cookies to cool on baking sheet for 5 minutes before removing to a wire rack to cool completely.

Chocolate Cookies

Ingredients

1 cup confectioners' sugar

¼ cup unsweetened cocoa powder

⅛ teaspoon salt

2 large egg whites

1 teaspoon vanilla extract

½ cup bittersweet chocolate chips or chunks, chopped

Directions

Preheat oven to 350°F. Line 2 large baking sheets with parchment paper. Coat the paper with cooking spray.

Combine confectioners' sugar, cocoa powder and salt in a medium bowl. Beat egg whites in a large mixing bowl with an electric mixer until soft peaks form. Add vanilla. Fold in the cocoa powder mixture with a rubber spatula until combined. Fold in chocolate chips (or chunks).

Drop the batter by tablespoonfuls onto the prepared baking sheets, leaving about 2 inches between each cookie.

Bake, one sheet at a time, until the cookies are just beginning to crack on top, 12 to 14 minutes. Let cool slightly on the pan before transferring to a wire rack to cool completely.

Oatmeal Apple Cookies

Ingredients

1 cup all-purpose flour

1 teaspoon baking powder

1 teaspoon ground cinnamon

1/2 teaspoon salt

1/2 teaspoon ground nutmeg

1/2 cup shortening

3/4 cup white sugar

2 eggs

1 cup rolled oats

1 cup diced apple without peel

1 cup chopped walnuts

Directions

Preheat oven to 350 degrees F (175 degrees C).

In a large bowl, cream together the shortening and sugar. Beat in the eggs until well blended. Combine the flour, baking powder, cinnamon, nutmeg, and salt; stir into the sugar mixture until well blended. Fold in the walnuts, oats and apples. Drop dough by spoonfuls about 2 inches onto ungreased cookie sheets.

Bake for 12 to 15 minutes in the preheated oven. Let cool on wire racks.

Oatmeal Peanut Butter Cookies

Ingredients

1/2 cup shortening

1/2 cup margarine, softened

1 cup packed brown sugar

3/4 cup white sugar

1 cup peanut butter

2 eggs

1 1/2 cups all-purpose flour

2 teaspoons baking soda

1 teaspoon salt

1 cup quick-cooking oats

Directions

Preheat oven to 350 degrees F (175 degrees C).

In a large bowl, cream together shortening, margarine, brown sugar, white sugar, and peanut butter until smooth. Beat in the eggs one at a time until well blended. Combine the flour, baking soda, and salt; stir into the creamed mixture. Mix in the oats until just combined. Drop by teaspoonfuls onto ungreased cookie sheets.

Bake for 10 to 15 minutes in the preheated oven, or until just light brown. Don't over-bake. Cool and store in an airtight container.

Molasses Sugar Cookies

Ingredients

1 1/2 cups shortening

2 cups white sugar

1/2 cup molasses

2 eggs

4 cups all-purpose flour

4 teaspoons baking soda

2 teaspoons ground cinnamon

1 teaspoon ground cloves

1 teaspoon ground ginger

1 teaspoon salt

Directions

Melt the shortening in a large pan on the stove, and cool.

Add sugar, eggs, and molasses, beat well. In a separate bowl, sift dry ingredients together and add to the pan. Mix well and chill 3 hours or overnight.

Form into walnut-size balls. Roll in granulated sugar. Place on greased cookie sheet about 2 inches apart. Bake at 375 degrees F (190 degrees C) for 8-10 minutes.

Sugar Cookies

Ingredients

2 3/4 cups all-purpose flour

1 teaspoon baking soda

1/2 teaspoon salt

1 1/4 cups margarine

2 cups white sugar

2 eggs

2 teaspoons vanilla extract

1/4 cup white sugar for decoration

Directions

Preheat oven to 350 degrees F (175 degrees C). In a medium bowl, stir together the flour, baking soda, and salt; set aside.

In a large bowl, cream together the margarine and 2 cups sugar until light and fluffy. Beat in the eggs one at a time, then the vanilla. Gradually stir in the dry ingredients until just blended. Roll the dough into walnut sized balls and roll the balls in remaining 1/4 cup of sugar. Place cookies 2 inches apart onto ungreased cookie sheets and flatten slightly.

Bake for 8 to 10 minutes in the preheated oven, until lightly browned at the edges. Allow cookies to cool on baking sheet for 5 minutes before removing to a wire rack to cool completely.

Oatmeal Banana Cookies

Ingredients

1 1/2 cups sifted all-purpose flour

1/2 teaspoon baking soda

1 teaspoon salt

1/4 teaspoon ground nutmeg

3/4 teaspoon ground cinnamon

3/4 cup shortening

1 cup white sugar

1 egg

1 cup mashed bananas

1 3/4 cups quick cooking oats

1/2 cup chopped nuts

Directions

Preheat oven to 400 degrees F (200 degrees C).

Sift together the flour, baking soda, salt, nutmeg and cinnamon.

Cream together the shortening and sugar; beat until light and fluffy. Add egg, banana, oatmeal and nuts. Mix well.

Add dry ingredients, mix well and drop by the teaspoon on ungreased cookie sheet.

Bake at 400 degrees F (200 degrees C) for 15 minutes or until edges turn lightly brown. Cool on wire rack. Store in a closed container.

Pumpkin Spice Cookies

Ingredients

⅔ cup whole-wheat pastry flour

⅔ cup all-purpose flour

1 teaspoon baking powder

½ teaspoon baking soda

½ teaspoon salt

1 teaspoon ground cinnamon

½ teaspoon ground ginger

¼ teaspoon ground allspice

¼ teaspoon freshly grated nutmeg

2 large eggs

¾ cup packed light brown sugar

¾ cup canned unseasoned pumpkin puree

¼ cup canola oil

¼ cup dark molasses

1 cup raisins

Directions

Preheat oven to 350°F. Coat 3 baking sheets with cooking spray.

Whisk whole-wheat flour, all-purpose flour, baking powder, baking soda, salt, cinnamon, ginger, allspice and nutmeg in a large bowl. Whisk eggs, brown sugar, pumpkin, oil and molasses in a second bowl until well combined. Stir the wet ingredients and raisins into the dry ingredients until thoroughly combined.

Drop the batter by level tablespoonfuls onto the prepared baking sheets, spacing the cookies 1½ inches apart.

Bake the cookies until firm to the touch and lightly golden on top, switching the pans back to front and top to bottom halfway through, 10 to 12 minutes. Transfer to a wire rack to cool.

Classic Peanut Butter Cookies

Ingredients

1 cup peanut butter

1 cup white sugar

1 egg

Directions

Preheat oven to 350 degrees F (175 degrees C). Line baking sheets with parchment paper.

Combine the peanut butter, white sugar and egg. Mix until smooth.

Drop spoonfuls of dough onto the prepared baking sheet. Bake at 350 F (175 degrees C) for 6 to 8 minutes.

Chocolate Crinkle Cookies

Ingredients

1 cup unsweetened cocoa powder

2 cups white sugar

1/2 cup vegetable oil

4 eggs

2 teaspoons vanilla extract

2 cups all-purpose flour

2 teaspoons baking powder

1/2 teaspoon salt

1/2 cup confectioners' sugar

Directions

In a medium bowl, mix together cocoa, white sugar, and vegetable oil. Beat in eggs one at a time, then stir in the vanilla. Combine the flour, baking powder, and salt; stir into the cocoa mixture. Cover dough, and chill for at least 4 hours.

Preheat oven to 350 degrees F (175 degrees C). Line cookie sheets with parchment paper. Roll dough into one inch balls. I like to use a number 50 size scoop. Coat each ball in confectioners' sugar before placing onto prepared cookie sheets.

Bake in preheated oven for 10 to 12 minutes. Let stand on the cookie sheet for a minute before transferring to wire racks to cool.

Peanut Butter Balls

Ingredients

½ cup natural peanut butter, almond butter or sunflower nut butter

¾ cup rolled oats

1 teaspoon pure maple syrup

½ cup dark chocolate chips, melted

Directions

Line a baking sheet with parchment or wax paper. Combine peanut butter, oats and maple syrup in a medium bowl. Roll the mixture into 12 balls, using about 2 teaspoons for each. Place the balls on the prepared baking sheet. Freeze until firm, about 15 minutes.

Roll the balls in melted chocolate. Return to the freezer until the chocolate is set, about 15 minutes.

Snickerdoodle Cookies

Ingredients

1 cup shortening

1 1/2 cups white sugar

2 eggs

2 3/4 cups all-purpose flour

1 teaspoon baking soda

2 teaspoons cream of tartar

1/2 teaspoon salt

2 tablespoons white sugar

2 teaspoons ground cinnamon

Directions

Preheat oven to 375 degrees F (190 degrees C).

In a medium bowl, cream together the shortening and 1 1/2 cups sugar. Stir in the eggs. Sift together the flour, baking soda, cream of tartar, and salt; stir into the creamed mixture until well blended. In a small bowl, stir together the 2 tablespoons of sugar, and the cinnamon.

Roll dough into walnut sized balls, then roll the balls in the cinnamon-sugar. Place them onto an unprepared cookie sheet, two inches apart.

Bake for 8 to 10 minutes in the preheated oven. Edges should be slightly brown. Remove from sheets to cool on wire racks.

Almond Cookies

Ingredients

Nonstick cooking spray

2¼ cups whole almonds

¾ cup sugar or sugar substitute blend equivalent to ¾ cup sugar

2 egg whites

1 teaspoon almond extract or vanilla

31 almond slices (2 tablespoons)

2 ounces bittersweet chocolate, melted

Directions

Preheat oven to 350°F. Line 2 large cookie sheets with parchment paper or coat with nonstick cooking spray; set aside. In a food processor, combine whole almonds and sugar; cover and process until finely ground. Add egg whites and almond extract. Cover and process until well mixed.

Using a well-rounded teaspoonful of the almond mixture for each cookie, shape into a crescent shape or ball. Place 1 inch apart on prepared cookie sheets. Place an almond slice on top of each cookie.

Bake for 10 to 12 minutes or until cookies are starting to brown on the tops. Transfer to wire racks; let cool. If desired, transfer the warm melted chocolate to a resealable plastic bag.

Seal bag; cut a small hole in one corner. Drizzle tops of cookies with melted chocolate.

Chapter 2: Dairy Free Cake And Square Recipes

Walnut Brownies

Ingredients

3/4 cup blanched almond flour

2/3 cup agave nectar

1/2 cup chopped walnuts (optional)

2 eggs

5 tablespoons unsweetened cocoa powder

1/4 cup coconut oil

1 teaspoon vanilla extract

Directions

Preheat oven to 350 degrees F (175 degrees C).

Mix almond flour, agave nectar, walnuts, eggs, cocoa powder, coconut oil, and vanilla extract together in a bowl; spread into an 8-inch square baking dish.

Bake in the preheated oven until edges of brownies begin to pull from sides of dish, about 30 minutes. Let brownies cool slightly before slicing, about 5 minutes.

Sponge Cake

Ingredients

1 2/3 cups all-purpose flour

1 1/2 teaspoons baking powder

1/2 teaspoon salt

3/4 cup egg yolks

1 egg

1 1/2 cups white sugar

1 tablespoon orange zest

1 tablespoon orange juice, strained

1/2 teaspoon lemon extract

3/4 cup boiling water

Directions

Preheat oven to 325 degrees F (165 degrees C).

Sift together twice: flour, baking powder, and salt. Pour back into sifter.

In a large mixing bowl beat egg yolks and whole eggs with an electric mixer until thick and lemon colored (about 5 minutes). Gradually add sugar, beating after each addition. This should take about 10 minutes.

Fold in orange rind, orange juice, and lemon extract. Sift dry ingredients into egg and sugar mixture and fold in. Do not stir or beat. Add boiling water and fold in quickly, just until liquid is blended. Pour batter into one ungreased 10 inch tube pan.

Bake at 325 degrees F (165 degrees C) for 60 to 65 minutes. Turn cake over in pan on a wire rack and let cake hang for 1 hour or until cool.

Loosen cake sides from pan with a spatula and shake from pan. Dust top lightly with confectioner's sugar or frost with Orange Butter Frosting.

Apple Cake

Ingredients

2 cups apples - peeled, cored and diced

1 tablespoon white sugar

1 teaspoon ground cinnamon

3 cups all-purpose flour

3 teaspoons baking powder

1/2 teaspoon salt

2 cups white sugar

1 cup vegetable oil

1/4 cup orange juice

2 1/2 teaspoons vanilla extract

4 eggs

1 cup chopped walnuts

1/4 cup confectioners' sugar for dusting

Directions

Preheat oven to 350 degrees F (175 degrees C). Grease and flour a 10 inch Bundt or tube pan. In a medium bowl, combine the diced apples, 1 tablespoon white sugar and 1 teaspoon cinnamon; set aside. Sift together the flour, baking powder and salt; set aside.

In a large bowl, combine 2 cups white sugar, oil, orange juice, vanilla and eggs. Beat at high speed until smooth. Stir in flour mixture. Fold in chopped walnuts.

Pour 1/3 of the batter into prepared pan. Sprinkle with 1/2 of the apple mixture. Alternate layers of batter and filling, ending with batter.

Bake in preheated oven for 55 to 60 minutes, or until the top springs back when lightly touched.

Let cool in pan for 10 minutes, then turn out onto a wire rack and cool completely. Sprinkle with confectioners' sugar.

Honey Cake

Ingredients

1 cup white sugar

1 cup honey

1/2 cup vegetable oil

4 eggs

2 teaspoons grated orange zest

1 cup orange juice

2 1/2 cups all-purpose flour

3 teaspoons baking powder

1/2 teaspoon baking soda

1/2 teaspoon salt

1 teaspoon ground cinnamon

Directions

Preheat oven to 350 degrees F (175 degrees C). Grease and flour a 9x13 inch pan.

Sift together the flour, baking powder, baking soda, salt and cinnamon. Set aside.

In a large bowl, combine sugar, honey, oil, eggs and orange zest. Beat in the flour mixture alternately with the orange juice, mixing just until incorporated. Pour batter into prepared pan.

Bake in the preheated oven for 40 to 50 minutes, or until a toothpick inserted into the center of the cake comes out clean. Allow to cool.

Pumpkin Cake

Ingredients

1 cup vegetable oil

3 eggs

1 (15 ounce) can pumpkin puree

1 teaspoon vanilla extract

2 1/2 cups white sugar

2 1/2 cups all-purpose flour

1 teaspoon baking soda

1 teaspoon ground nutmeg

1 teaspoon ground allspice

1 teaspoon ground cinnamon

1 teaspoon ground cloves

1/4 teaspoon salt

1 cup chopped walnuts

Directions

Preheat oven to 350 degrees F (175 degrees C). Grease one 10-inch bundt or tube pan.

Blend oil, beaten eggs, pumpkin and vanilla together.

Sift the flour, sugar, baking soda, ground nutmeg, ground allspice, ground cinnamon, ground cloves and salt together. Add the flour mixture to the pumpkin mixture and mix until just combined. If desired, stir in some chopped nuts. Pour batter into the prepared pan.

Bake in preheated oven until a toothpick inserted in the middle comes out clean, about 1 hour.

Let cake cool in pan for 5 minutes, then turn out onto a plate and sprinkle with confectioners' sugar.

Peanut Butter Brownies

Ingredients

1/2 cup peanut butter

1/3 cup margarine, softened

2/3 cup white sugar

1/2 cup packed brown sugar

2 egg

1/2 teaspoon vanilla extract

1 cup all-purpose flour

1 teaspoon baking powder

1/4 teaspoon salt

Directions

Preheat oven to 350 degrees F (175 degrees C). Grease a 9x9 inch baking pan.

In a medium bowl, cream together peanut butter and margarine. Gradually blend in the brown sugar, white sugar, eggs, and vanilla; mix until fluffy. Combine flour, baking powder, and salt; stir into the peanut butter mixture until well blended.

Bake for 30 to 35 minutes in preheated oven, or until the top springs back when touched. Cool, and cut into 16 squares.

Molasses Cinnamon Cake

Ingredients

1/2 cup shortening

1/2 cup packed brown sugar

1 cup molasses

2 eggs

1/2 teaspoon salt

1 teaspoon ground cinnamon

1/2 teaspoon ground cloves

1 teaspoon ground ginger

2 1/2 cups all-purpose flour

1 teaspoon baking soda

1 cup hot, brewed coffee

Directions

Sift together salt, cinnamon, cloves, ginger, flour, and baking soda.

Cream shortening and sugar gradually, then add molasses and eggs. Mix in sifted ingredients. Stir in hot coffee; batter will be thin.

Bake at 350 degrees F (175 degrees C) for 30 minutes. Cool.

Pear Cake

Ingredients

4 cups peeled, cored and chopped pears

2 cups white sugar

3 cups sifted all-purpose flour

1 teaspoon salt

1 1/2 teaspoons baking soda

1 teaspoon ground nutmeg

1 teaspoon ground cinnamon

1/2 teaspoon ground cloves

4 egg whites

2/3 cup canola oil

1 cup chopped pecans

Directions

Combine the pears and the sugar and let stand for one hour.

Preheat oven to 325 degrees F (165 degrees C). Spray a 10 inch bundt pan with non-stick cooking spray.

Slightly beat the egg whites and combine them with the oil, chopped pecans and pear mixture.

Stir the flour, salt, baking soda, nutmeg, cinnamon and cloves. Stir in the pear mixture. Pour batter into the prepared bundt pan.

Bake at 325 degrees F (165 degrees C) for 1 hour and 10 minutes. Remove from oven and let cool on a wire rack for 10 minutes before removing from pan.

Citrus Cake

Ingredients

1½ cups cake flour

1½ cups granulated sugar, divided

1 teaspoon baking powder

¼ teaspoon salt

10 large egg whites, at room temperature

½ teaspoon cream of tartar

3 large large egg yolks

2 tablespoons Grand Marnier or other orange liqueur

2 tablespoons freshly grated orange zest

2 teaspoons freshly grated lemon zest

2 teaspoons freshly grated lime zest

1 tablespoon lemon juice

1 tablespoon lime juice

1 teaspoon vanilla extract

Glaze

1 large orange

1 lemon, scrubbed

1 lime, scrubbed

2 cups confectioners' sugar

Directions

To make cake:

Preheat oven to 350°F. Sift flour, ¾ cup granulated sugar, baking powder and salt into a small bowl; set aside.

Beat egg whites and cream of tartar in the bowl of an electric mixer just until soft peaks form. Beat in the remaining ¾ cup granulated sugar, 2 tablespoons at a time, until the whites are shiny and form soft peaks.

Whisk together egg yolks, orange liqueur, orange, lemon and lime zests, lemon and lime juices, and vanilla in a small bowl. Pour over the egg whites and fold together with a rubber spatula.

Resift the reserved dry ingredients over the beaten egg whites in four parts, folding in gently after each addition. Spoon the batter into an ungreased 10-inch angel food cake pan with a removable bottom. Smooth the top and run a knife or spatula through the batter to remove any air bubbles.

Bake until the top is golden and a long skewer inserted into the cake comes out clean, 45 to 50 minutes. Invert the pan over the neck of a bottle and let cool completely.

To make citrus glaze:

Use a citrus zester to remove long threads of zest from the orange, lemon and lime; set aside. Squeeze 4 teaspoons of juice from each of the fruits. Whisk the juices into the confectioners' sugar in a small bowl to make a smooth glaze.

Loosen the edges of the cake with a knife and invert onto a cake plate. Spoon the glaze over the top, allowing it to drip down the sides. Sprinkle the top of the cake with the julienned zest. Let the cake stand at least 30 minutes for the glaze to set.

Almond Cake

Ingredients

1½ cups whole almonds, toasted

4 large eggs, at room temperature, separated

½ cup honey

1 teaspoon vanilla extract

½ teaspoon baking soda

½ teaspoon salt

Topping

2 tablespoons honey

¼ cup sliced almonds, toasted

Ingredients

Preheat oven to 350°F. Coat a 9-inch springform pan with cooking spray. Line the bottom with parchment paper and spray the paper.

Process whole almonds in a food processor or blender until finely ground. Beat 4 egg yolks, ½ cup honey, vanilla, baking soda and salt in a large mixing bowl with an electric mixer on medium speed until well combined. Add the ground almonds and beat on low until combined.

Beat 4 egg whites in another large bowl with the electric mixer on medium speed until very foamy, white and doubled in volume, but not stiff enough to hold peaks, 1 to 2 minutes. Using a rubber spatula, gently fold the egg whites into the nut mixturee until just combined. Scrape the batter into the prepared pan.

Bake the cake until golden brown and a skewer inserted into the center comes out clean, 25 to 28 minutes. Let cool in the pan for 10 minutes. Run a knife around the edge of the pan and gently remove the side ring. Let cool completely.

If desired, remove the cake from the pan bottom by gently sliding a large, wide spatula between the cake and the parchment paper. Carefully transfer the cake to a serving platter. To serve, drizzle the top of the cake with honey and sprinkle with sliced almonds.

Zucchini Brownies

Ingredients
2 cups all-purpose flour

1 teaspoon salt

1 1/2 teaspoons baking soda

1/3 cup unsweetened cocoa powder

1 cup white sugar

2 eggs

2 cups grated zucchini

1/2 cup vegetable oil

1 teaspoon vanilla extract

1/2 cup chopped walnuts

Directions
Preheat oven to 350 degrees F (175 degrees C). Grease a 10x15 inch jellyroll pan.

In a large mixing bowl, sift together flour, salt, soda, cocoa, and sugar. Combine eggs, zucchini, oil, and vanilla; blend into dry ingredients. Stir in walnuts.

Bake for 20 minutes in preheated oven. Cool in the pan, and then cut into bars.

Chocolate Cake

Ingredients

1 1/2 cups sifted pastry flour

1 cup white sugar

1/4 cup unsweetened cocoa powder

1 teaspoon baking powder

1 teaspoon baking soda

1/4 teaspoon salt

1 cup water

1/3 cup vegetable oil

1/4 cup white vinegar

1 teaspoon vanilla extract

Directions

Preheat oven to 350 degrees F (175 degrees C). Use a un-greased 8 inch square pan.

Sift together the flour, sugar, cocoa, baking powder, baking soda and salt into an un-greased pan. Make a well in the center and pour in the water, oil, vinegar and vanilla. Mix until blended.

Bake in the preheated oven for 25 to 30 minutes, or until a toothpick inserted into the center of the cake comes out clean. Allow to cool.

Hazelnut Chocolate Cake

Ingredients

½ cup chopped pitted dates

½ cup unsweetened cocoa powder

1 teaspoon instant coffee granules

½ cup boiling water

½ cup chopped hazelnuts, plus 2 tablespoons for garnish

2 slices firm white bread, crusts trimmed

⅓ cup all-purpose flour

¼ teaspoon salt

⅔ cup sugar, divided

2 tablespoons canola oil

1 teaspoon vanilla extract

1 large egg

3 large egg whites

Glaze

⅓ cup unsweetened cocoa powder

2 ounces bittersweet (not unsweetened) chocolate, finely chopped (⅓ cup)

1 tablespoon corn syrup

1 teaspoon instant coffee granules

¼ cup boiling water

½ teaspoon vanilla extract

1 cup confectioners' sugar

Directions

To make cake: Preheat oven to 350°F. Coat a 9-inch round cake pan with cooking spray. Line the bottom with parchment or wax paper.

Combine dates, cocoa and instant coffee in a small bowl. Add boiling water and stir until the cocoa has dissolved. Cover and let stand until the dates have softened and the mixture has cooled to room temperature, about 20 minutes.

Spread hazelnuts in a shallow baking dish and bake until fragrant and lightly toasted, 5 to 10 minutes. Transfer to a plate and let cool.

Grind bread into fine crumbs in a food processor. Measure to make sure you have ½ cup. Transfer to a large bowl.

Place ½ cup of the hazelnuts in the food processor. Add flour and salt; process until the nuts are finely ground. Transfer to the bowl with the breadcrumbs.

Scrape the cooled date mixture into the food processor. Add ⅓ cup sugar, oil, vanilla and whole egg; process until smooth, stopping several times to scrape down the sides of the bowl. Scrape the mixture into the bowl with the breadcrumbs and nuts. Mix gently with a rubber spatula.

Beat egg whites with an electric mixer in a clean large mixing bowl until soft peaks form. Gradually add remaining ⅓ cup sugar, beating until stiff, glossy peaks form. Add one-fourth of the beaten whites to the batter and whisk until blended. Fold in the remaining whites with a rubber spatula just until blended. Scrape the batter into the prepared pan, spreading evenly.

Bake the cake until the top springs back when touched lightly, 25 to 35 minutes. Let cool in the pan on a wire rack for 5 minutes. Coat the rack with cooking spray and invert the cake onto it to cool completely.

To make glaze:

Combine cocoa, chocolate, corn syrup and instant coffee in a medium bowl. Add boiling water and stir with a wooden spoon until the chocolate has melted and the mixture is smooth. Stir in vanilla. Gradually add confectioners' sugar, beating with an electric mixer, slowly at first, then gradually increasing speed, until the glaze is smooth and thickened. Cover with plastic wrap and let sit at room temperature until the mixture is set, about 30 minutes.

To finish the cake, place it bottom-side up on a serving plate. Place several strips of wax paper under the bottom edge to protect the plate from drips.

Spoon on glaze and spread it evenly over the top and sides of the cake with an icing spatula or knife. Arrange the remaining 2 tablespoons hazelnuts around the top outside edge. Discard the wax paper before serving.

Printed in Poland
by Amazon Fulfillment
Poland Sp. z o.o., Wrocław